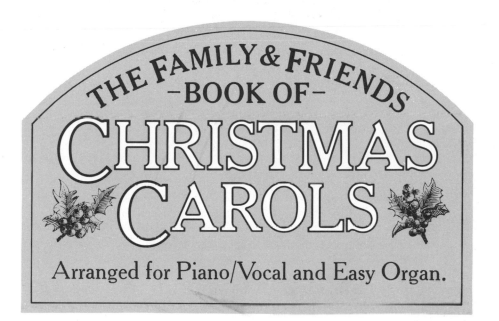

THE FAMILY & FRIENDS
—BOOK OF—
CHRISTMAS CAROLS

Arranged for Piano/Vocal and Easy Organ.

Wise Publications
London/New York/Sydney

Exclusive distributors:
Music Sales Limited,
78 Newman Street, London W1P 3LA, England.
Music Sales Pty. Limited,
27 Clarendon Street, Artarmon, Sydney, NSW 2064, Australia.
Music Sales Corp.,
33 West 60th Street, New York 10023, New York, U.S.A.

This book © Copyright 1977 by
Wise Publications
ISBN 0.86001.436.3
AM 1973T

All songs © Copyright 1977 by Dorsey Bros. Music Ltd.,
78 Newman Street, London W1P 3LA,
except 'Pa Rum Pa Pum Pum', © Copyright 1961 Encore Publications Inc.
1619 Broadway, New York, N.Y. Tristan Music Ltd., London

Music compiled by Cathy Lewis
Book design by Howard Brown
Cover illustration by Graham Percy

Printed in England by
Newmeirprint Limited, London

Music Sales complete catalogue lists thousands of titles
and is free from your local Music Book shop
or direct from Music Sales Limited.
Please send 15p in stamps for postage to
Music Sales Limited, 78 Newman Street, London W1P 3LA.

Angels From The Realms Of Glory

(For Organ: Registration No. 3)

Fairly slow

1. An - gels, from the realms of glo - ry / Wing your flight o'er all the earth; / Ye who sang cre - a - tion's sto - ry, / Now pro - claim Mes - si - ah's birth.

2. Shep - herds in the fields a - bi - ding, / Watch - ing o'er your flocks by night; / God with man is now re - si - ding; / Yon - der shines the in - fant light.

CHORUS

Come and wor - ship, wor - ship Christ the new - born King.

3. Sages leave your contemplations,
    Brighter visions beam afar;
    Seek the great desire of nations,
    Ye have seen His natal star.
        Come and worship etc.

4. Saints, before the altar bending
    Watching long with hope and fear,
    Suddenly the Lord, descending,
    In His temple shall appear;
        Come and worship etc.

5. Sinner, wrung with true repentance,
    Doomed for guilt to endless pains,
    Justice now revokes the sentence —
    Mercy calls you — break your chains.
        Come and worship etc.

5

As With Gladness Men Of Old

Words by William C. Dix. Music by W. H. Monk.

(For Organ: Registration No. 7)

3. As they offered gifts most rare
    At Thy cradle rude and bare,
    So may we with holy joy,
    Pure and free from sin's alloy,
    All our costliest treasures bring,
    Christ, to Thee, our heavenly King.

4. Holy Jesus, ev'ry day
    Keep us in the narrow way;
    And when earthly things are past,
    Bring our ransomed souls at last
    Where they need no star to guide,
    Where no clouds Thy glory hide.

Away In A Manger

(For Organ: Registration No. 7)

3.   Be near me, Lord Jesus;
I ask Thee to stay
Close by me forever,
And love me, I pray.
Bless all the dear children
In Thy tender care,
And fit us for heaven,
To live with Thee there.

Christmas Is Coming

English

(For Organ: Registration No. 5)

Allegro moderato

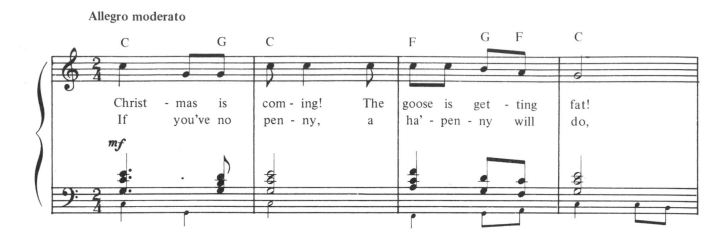

Christ - mas is com - ing! The goose is get - ting fat!
If you've no pen - ny, a ha' - pen - ny will do,

Please to put a pen - ny in an old man's ___ hat,
If you have no ha - pen - ny, then God bless ___ you,

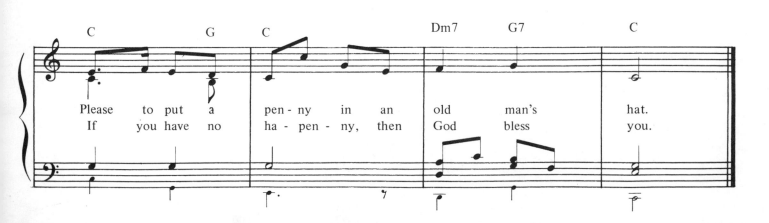

Please to put a pen - ny in an old man's hat.
If you have no ha - pen - ny, then God bless you.

Christ Was Born On Christmas Day

German

(For Organ: Registration No. 2)

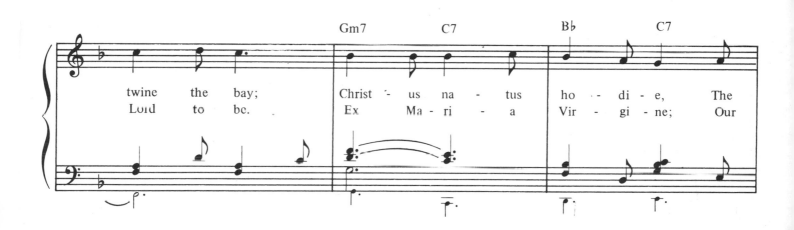

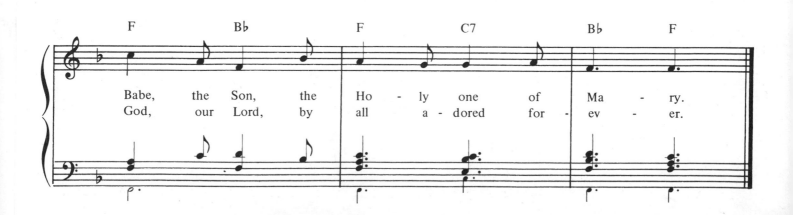

Ding Dong Merrily On High

(For Organ: Registration No. 2)

Brightly

1. Ding dong! mer-ri-ly on high The bells are gai-ly ring-ing.
2. Ding dong! car-ol all the bells. A-wake not, do not tar-ry!

Ding dong! hap-pi-ly re-ply The an-gels all a-sing-ing.
Sing out, sound the good Now-ells, Je-su is born of Ma-ry.

Glo - - - - - - ri-a, Ho-san-na in ex-cel-sis!

3.   Ring out, merry merry bells,
The Angels all are singing.
Ding dong! swing the steep bells,
Sound joyous news we're bringing!
     Gloria etc.

4.   Hark now! happily we sing,
The Angels wish us merry!
Ding dong! dancing as we bring
Good news from Virgin Mary.
     Gloria etc.

Good Christian Men Rejoice

(For Organ: Registration No. 2)

3. Good Christian men, rejoice
    With heart and soul and voice;
    Now ye need not fear the grave:
        Peace! Peace!
    Jesus Christ was born to save!
    Calls you one and calls you all,
    To gain His everlasting hall:
        Christ was born to save!
        Christ was born to save!

The First Nowell

(For Organ: Registration No. 4)

1. The first No - well the an - gels did
2. They look - ed up and saw a

say, was to cer - tain poor shep - herds in fields as they
star, was shi - ning in the east be - yond them

lay; in fields where they lay keep - ing their
far, and to the earth it gave great

sheep, on a cold win - ter's night that was so deep.
light and so it con - tin - ued both day and night.

Now

CHORUS

3. And by the light of that same star,
   Three wise men came from country far;
   To seek for a king was their intent,
   And to follow the star wherever it went.
        Nowell etc.

4. This star drew nigh to the north-west,
   O'er Bethlehem it took its rest,
   And there it did both stop and stay,
   Right over the place where Jesus lay.
        Nowell etc.

5. Then let us all with one accord,
   Sing praises to our heavenly Lord,
   That hath made heaven and earth of nought,
   And with His blood mankind hath bought.
        Nowell etc.

God Rest You Merry Gentlemen

(F or Organ: Registration No. 2)

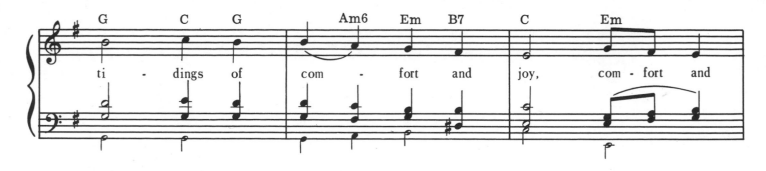

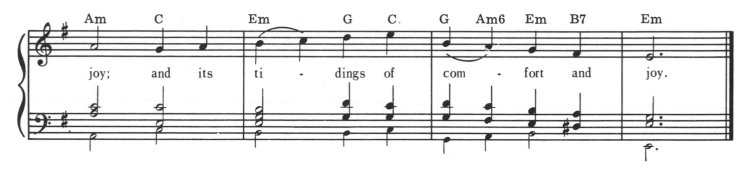

3. Go, fear not, said God's Angels,
    Let nothing you affright,
    For there is born in Bethlehem,
    Of a pure Virgin bright,
    One able to advance you,
    And throw down Satan quite.
        And its tidings etc.

4. The shepherds at those tidings,
    Rejoiced much in mind,
    And left their flocks a-feeding
    In tempest storms of wind,
    And straight they came to Bethlehem,
    The son of God to find.
        And its tidings etc.

5. Now when they came to Bethlehem,
    Where our sweet Saviour lay,
    They found him in a manger,
    Where oxen feed on hay,
    The blessed Virgin kneeling down,
    Unto the Lord did pray.
        And its tidings etc.

6. With sudden joy and gladness
    The shepherds were beguil'd,
    To see the babe of Israel
    Before His mother mild.
    On them with joy and cheerfulness
    Rejoice each mother's child.
        And its tidings etc.

7. Now to the Lord sing praises,
    All you within this place;
    Like we true loving brethren,
    Each other to embrace,
    For the merry time of Christmas
    Is drawing on apace.
        And its tidings etc.

Good King Wenceslas

(For Organ: Registration No. 5)

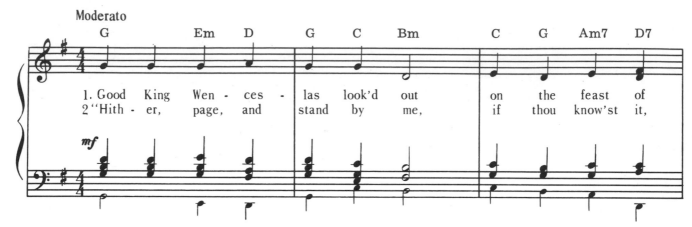

1. Good King Wen - ces - las look'd out on the feast of
2. "Hith - er, page, and stand by me, if thou know'st it,

Ste - phen, When the snow lay round a - bout
tell - ing Yon - der pea - sant, who is he?

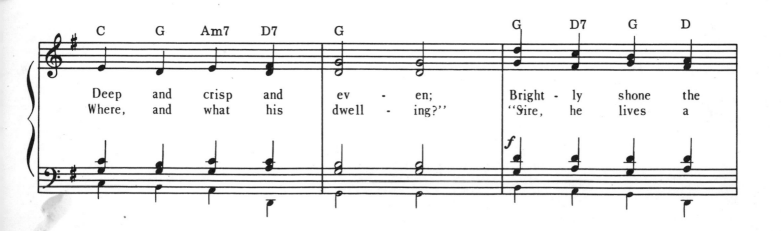

Deep and crisp and ev - en; Bright - ly shone the
Where, and what his dwell - ing?" "Sire, he lives a

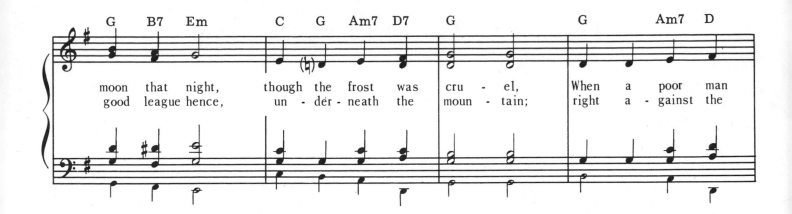

moon that night, though the frost was cru - el, When a poor man
good league hence, un - der - neath the moun - tain; right a - gainst the

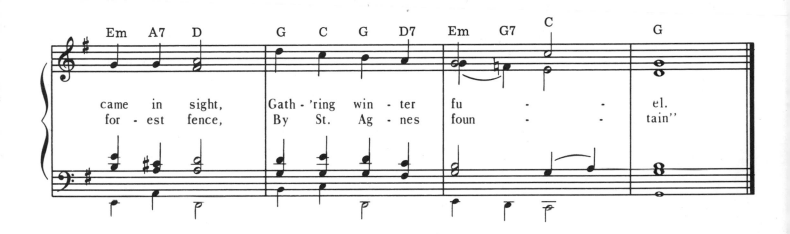

came in sight, Gath - 'ring win - ter fu - - el.
for - est fence, By St. Ag - nes foun - - tain"

3. "Bring me flesh and bring me wine,
   Bring me pine logs hither;
   Thou and I will see him dine,
   When we bear them thither."
   Page and monarch forth they went,
   Onward both together,
   Through the rude winds wild lament,
   And the bitter weather.

4. "Sire, the night is darker now
   And the wind blows stronger;
   Fails my heart, I know not how,
   I can go no longer."
   "Mark my footsteps, good my page!
   Tread thou in them boldly;
   Thou shall find the winter's rage
   Freeze thy blood less coldly."

5. In his master's steps he trod,
   Where the snow lay dinted;
   Heat was in the very sod
   Which the saint had printed.
   Therefore, Christian men, be sure —
   Wealth or rank possessing —
   Ye, who now will bless the poor,
   Shall yourselves find blessing.

Hark The Herald Angels Sing

(For Organ: Registration No. 5)

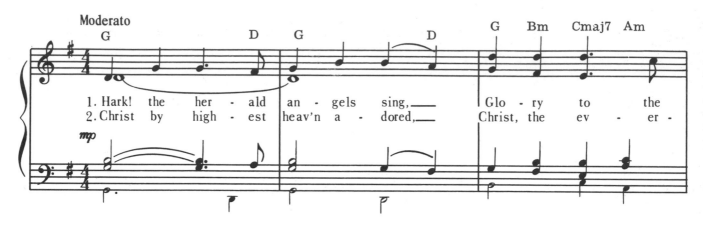

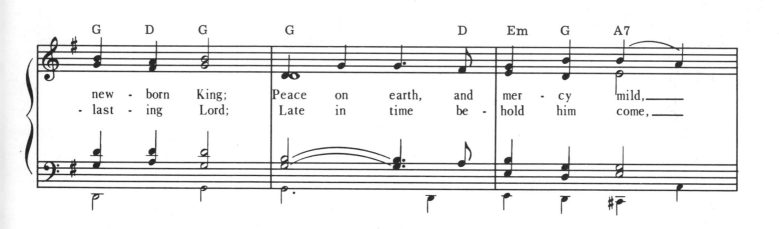

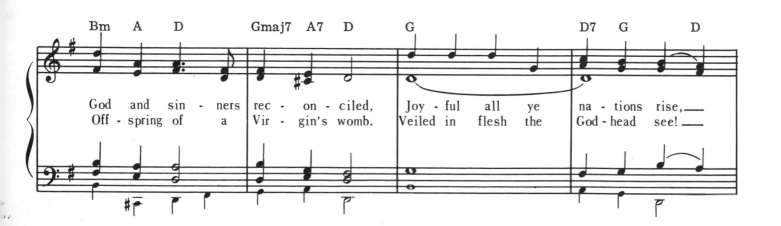

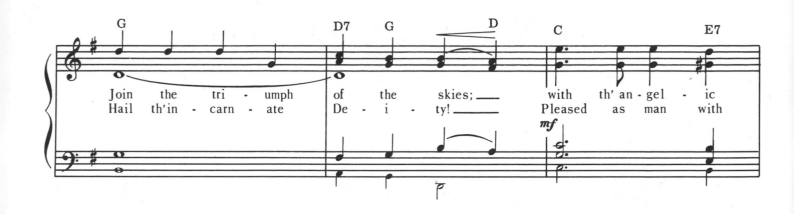

Join the tri - umph of the skies; ___ with th' an - gel - ic
Hail th'in - carn - ate De - i - ty! ___ Pleased as man with

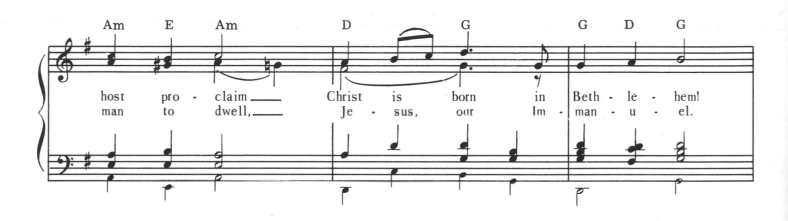

host pro - claim ___ Christ is born in Beth - le - hem!
man to dwell, ___ Je - sus, our Im - man - u - el.

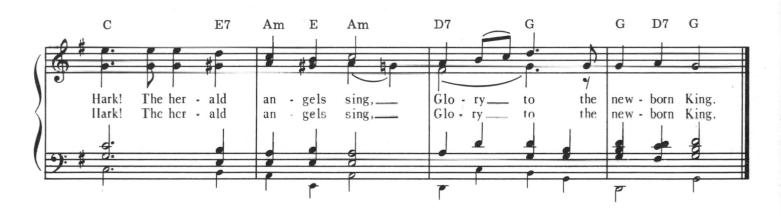

Hark! The her - ald an - gels sing, ___ Glo - ry ___ to the new - born King.
Hark! The her - ald an - gels sing, ___ Glo - ry ___ to the new - born King.

3. Hail, the heaven born Prince of peace!
    Hail, the Son of righteousness!
    Light and life to all He brings,
    Risen with healing in His wings,
    Mild He lays His glory by;
    Born that man no more may die;
    Born to raise the sons of earth;
    Born, to give them second birth.
        Hark! the herald angels sing,
        Glory to the new-born King!

Here We Come A Wassailing

(For Organ: Registration No. 2)

3.　Good Master and good Mistress,
　　As you sit by the fire,
　　Pray think of·us poor children
　　Who are wand'ring in the mire.
　　　　Love·and joy etc.

4.　God bless the Master of this house,
　　Likewise the Mistress too;
　　And all the little children
　　That round the table go.
　　　　Love and joy etc.

The Holly And The Ivy

(For Organ: Registration No. 4)

Fairly quick

1. The hol-ly and the i - vy, When they are both full grown, of __ all the trees that are
2. The hol-ly bears a blos-som, as white as the li - ly flower, and __ Ma-ry bore sweet

in the wood, the __ hol-ly bears the crown:
Je-sus Christ, to __ be our sweet sa - viour.

CHORUS

The ri-sing of the sun __ and the

run-ning of the deer, The __ play-ing of the mer-ry or-gan, sweet singing in the choir,

3. The holly bears a berry,
   As red as any blood,
   And Mary bore sweet Jesus Christ
   To do poor sinners good.
   The rising of etc.

4. The holly bears a prickle,
   As sharp as any thorn,
   And Mary bore sweet Jesus Christ
   On Christmas day in the morn.
   The rising of etc.

5. The holly bears a bark,
   As bitter as any gall,
   And Mary bore sweet Jesus Christ
   For to redeem us all.
   The rising of etc.

6. The holly and the ivy,
   When they are both full grown,
   Of all the trees that are in the wood,
   The holly bears the crown.
   The rising of etc.

It Came Upon The Midnight Clear

(For Organ: Registration No. 3)

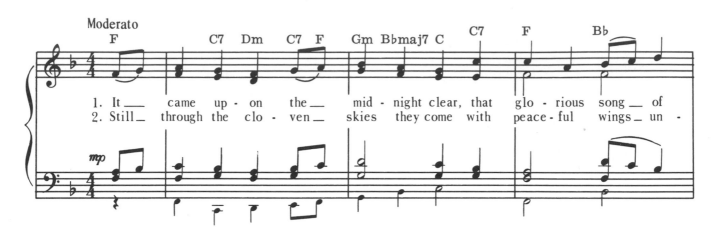

1. It __ came up - on the __ mid - night clear, that glo - rious song __ of
2. Still __ through the clo - ven __ skies they come with peace - ful wings __ un -

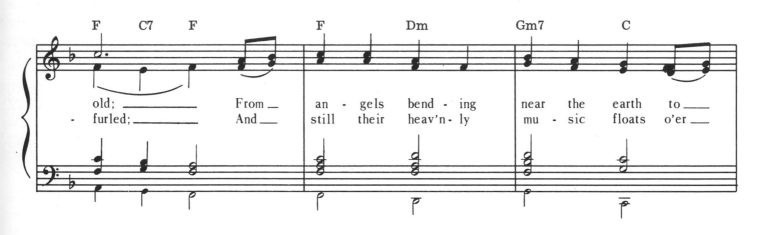

old; _____ From __ an - gels bend - ing near the earth to __
-furled; _____ And __ still their heav'n - ly mu - sic floats o'er __

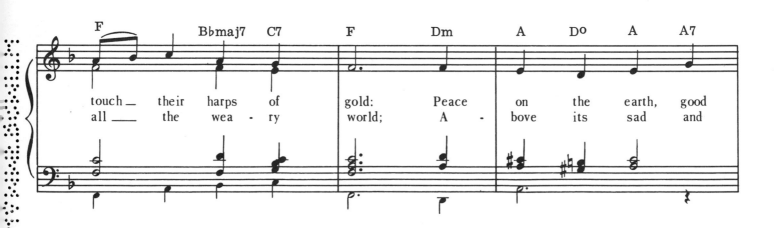

touch __ their harps of gold: Peace on the earth, good
all __ the wea - ry world; A - bove its sad and

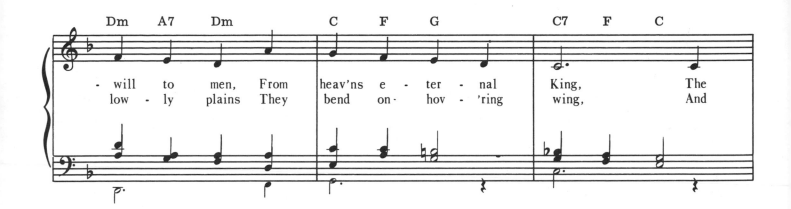

will   to   men,   From   heav'ns   e - ter - nal   King,   The
low - ly   plains   They   bend   on   hov - 'ring   wing,   And

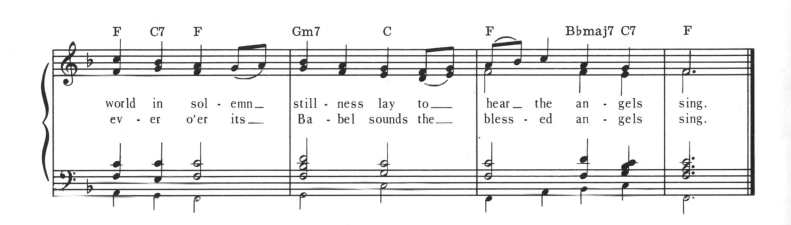

world   in   sol - emn   still - ness   lay   to   hear   the   an - gels   sing.
ev - er   o'er   its   Ba - bel   sounds   the   bless - ed   an - gels   sing.

3.   Yet with the woes of sin and strife
     The world has suffered long;
     Beneath the Angel-strain have rolled
     Two thousand years of wrong;
     And men, at war with men, hear not
     The love-song which they bring;
     Oh! hush the noise, ye men of strife
     And hear the angels sing!

4.   And ye, beneath life's crushing load,
     Whose forms are bending low,
     Who toil along the climbing way
     With painful steps and slow,
     Look now! for glad and golden hours
     Come swiftly on the wing;
     O rest beside the weary road
     And hear the Angels sing!

I Saw Three Ships

(For Organ: Registration No. 6)

3. The Virgin Mary and Christ were there,
    On Christmas day, on Christmas day:
    The Virgin Mary and Christ were there,
    On Christmas day in the morning.

4. Pray, whither sailed those ships all three,
    On Christmas day, on Christmas day?
    Pray whither sailed those ships all three,
    On Christmas day in the morning?

5. O they sailed into Bethlehem,
    On Christmas day, on Christmas day;
    O they sailed into Bethlehem,
    On Christmas day in the morning.

6. And all the bells on earth shall ring,
    On Christmas day, on Christmas day;
    And all the bells on earth shall ring,
    On Christmas day in the morning.

7. And all the Angels in heaven shall sing,
    On Christmas day, on Christmas day;
    And all the Angels in heaven shall sing,
    On Christmas day in the morning.

8. And all the souls on earth shall sing,
    On Christmas day, on Christmas day;
    And all the souls on earth shall sing,
    On Christmas day in the morning.

9. Then let us all rejoice again,
    On Christmas day, on Christmas day;
    Then let us all rejoice amain,
    On Christmas day in the morning.

Joy To The World

(For Organ: Registration No. 3)

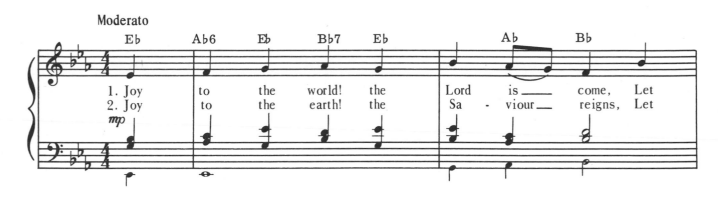

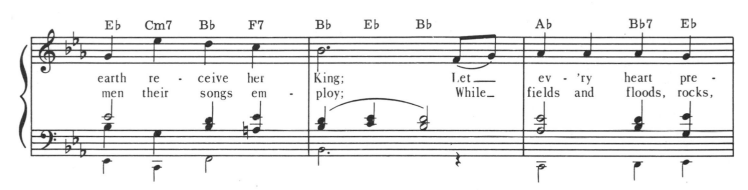

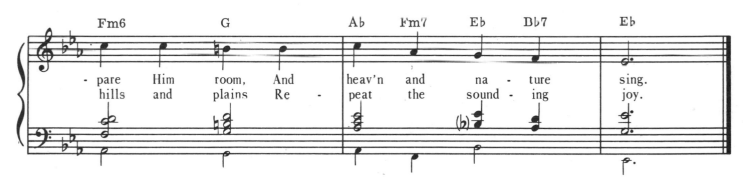

3. No more let sins and sorrows grow,
   Nor thorns infest the ground;
   He comes to make His blessings flow
   Far as the curse is found.

4. He rules the world with truth and grace,
   And makes the nations prove
   The glories of His righteousness,
   And wonders of His love.

Jingle Bells

Words and Music by James Pierpont

(For Organ: Registration No. 3)

3. Now the ground is white,
   Go it while you're young!
   Take the girls tonight,
   And sing this sleighing song.
   Just get a bobtail'd bay,
   Two forty for his speed,
   Then hitch him to an open sleigh
   And crack! You'll take the lead.
      Refrain:

O Tannenbaum (O Christmas Tree)

Old German

(For Organ: Registration No. 2)

2. O Christmas tree! O Christmas tree!
You are the tree most lovèd;
O Christmas tree! O Christmas tree!
You are the tree most lovèd;
How oft you've given me delight
When Christmas fires were burning bright!
O Christmas tree! O Christmas tree!
You are the tree most lovèd.

3. O Christmas tree! O Christmas tree!
Your faithful leaves will teach me
O Christmas tree! O Christmas tree!
Your faithful leaves will teach me
That hope and love and constancy
Give joy and peace eternally.
O Christmas tree! O Christmas tree!
Your faithful leaves will teach me.

O Come All Ye Faithful

(For Organ: Registration No. 4)

3. Sing, choirs of Angels,
   Sing in exultation,
   Sing, all ye citizens of heav'n above:
   'Glory to God in the highest;'
      O come, let us etc.

4. Yea, Lord, we greet Thee,
   Born this happy morning;
   Jesu, to Thee be glory given;
   Word of the Father, Now in flesh appearing;
      O come, let us etc.

O Holy Night

Words and Music by Adolphe Adam

(For Organ: Registration No. 6)

O Little Town Of Bethlehem

(For Organ: Registration No. 3)

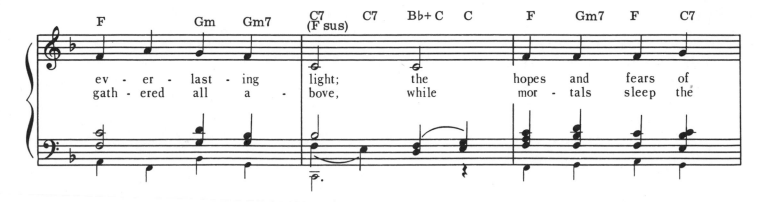

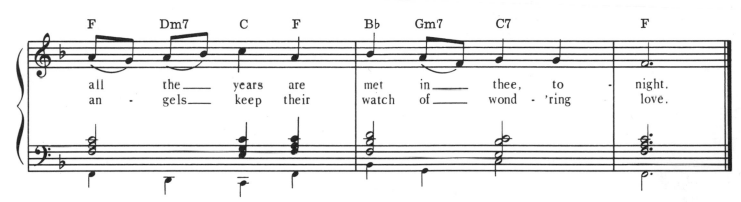

3. How silently, how silently,
The wondrous gift is given!
So God imparts to human hearts
The blessings of His heaven.
No ear may hear His coming;
But in this world of sin,
Where meek souls will receive Him, still
The dear Christ enters in.

4. Where children pure and happy
Pray to the blessed Child,
Where misery cries out to Thee,
Son of the mother mild;
Where charity stands watching
And faith holds wide the door,
The dark night wakes the glory breaks,
And Christmas comes once more.

5. O holy child of Bethlehem,
Descend to us we pray;
Cast out our sin and enter in,
Be born in us today.
We hear the Christmas Angels
The great glad tidings tell:
O come to us, abide with us,
Our Lord Emmanuel.

O Come, O Come Emmanuel

(For Organ: Registration No. 3)

French

3.   O come, Thou Day-Spring, come and cheer
    Our spirits by Thine advent here,
    Disperse the gloomy clouds of night,
    And death's dark shadows put to flight.
     Refrain:

4.   O come, Thou key to David come,
    And open wide our heav'nly home,
    Make safe the way that leads on high,
    And close the path to misery.
     Refrain:

Once in Royal David's City

(For Organ: Registration No. 3)

3. And through all His wondrous childhood,
   He would honour and obey,
   Love and watch the lowly Maiden
   In whose gentle arms He lay;
   Christian children all must be
   Mild, obedient, good as He.

4. For He is in our childhood's pattern,
   Day by day like us He grew;
   He was little, weak and helpless,
   Tears and smiles like us He knew;
   And He feeleth for our sadness,
   And He shareth in our gladness.

5. And our eyes at last shall see Him,
   Through His own redeeming love,
   For that Child so dear and gentle
   Is our Lord in heaven above;
   And he leads His children on
   To the place where He is gone.

6. Not in that poor lowly stable,
   With the oxen standing by,
   We shall see Him; but in heaven,
   Set at God's right hand on high;
   When like stars his children crown'd
   All in white shall wait around.

Pa Rum Pa Pum Pum

Words and Music by W. Hinderling

(For Organ: Registration No. 4)

Silent Night

(For Organ: Registration No. 7)

3. Silent night! holy night!
    Son of God, love's pure light;
    Radiant beams Thy holy face
    With the dawn of saving grace,
    Jesus, Lord, at Thy birth,
    Jesus, Lord, at Thy birth.

Twelve Days Of Christmas

(For Organ: Registration No. 5)

Unto Us A Boy Is Born

(For Organ: Registration No. 4)

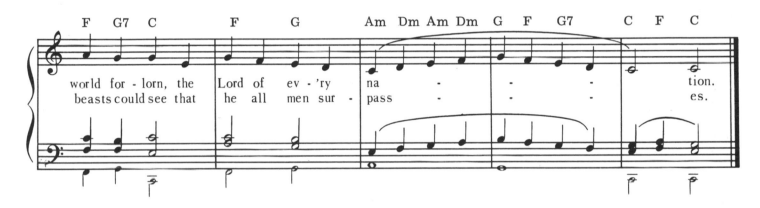

1. Un - to us a boy is born! King of all cre - a - tion, Came He to a world for - lorn, the Lord of ev - 'ry na - - - - tion.

2. Cra - dled in a stall was He with sleep-y cows and ass - es; But the ve - ry beasts could see that he all men sur - pass - - - - es.

3.   Herod then with fear was filled:
    "A prince", he said, "in Jewry!"
    All the little boys he killed
    At Bethlem in his fury.

4.   Now may Mary's son, who came
    So long ago to love us,
    Lead us all with hearts aflame
    Unto the joys above us.

5.   Omega and Alpha he!
    Let the organ thunder,
    While the choir with peals of glee
    Doth rend the air asunder.

We Three Kings

(For Organ: Registration No. 4)

(CASPAR)

3. Frankincense to offer have I;
    Incense owns a Deity nigh:
    Prayer and praising, all men raising,
    Worship him, God most high.
        O star of wonder etc.

(BALTHASAR)

4. Myrrh is mine; its bitter perfume
    Breathes a life of gathering gloom;
    Sorrowing, sighing, bleeding, dying,
    Sealed in the stone - cold tomb.
        O star of wonder etc.

(ALL)

5. Glorious now, behold him arise,
    King and God and Sacrifice!
    Heaven sings alleluya,
    Alleluya the earth replies.
        O star of wonder etc.

While Shepherds Watched Their Flocks

(For Organ: Registration No. 3)

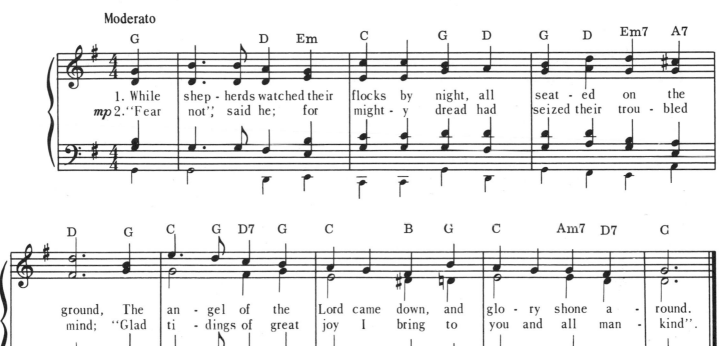

3. "To you in David's town this day
   Is born of David's line
   A Saviour, who is Christ the Lord;
   And this shall be the sign:

4. "The heavenly Babe you there shall find
   To human view displayed,
   All meanly wrapped in swathing bands
   And in a manger laid!"

5. Thus spake the Seraph; and forthwith
   Appeared a shining throng
   Of Angels praising God, who thus
   Addressed their joyful song:

6. "All glory be to God on high,
   And on the earth be peace;
   Good-will henceforth from heaven to men
   Begin and never cease."

We Wish You A Merry Christmas

(For Organ: Registration No. 6)

With spirit

Bb — **Eb** — **C7**

1. We wish you a mer-ry Christ-mas, We wish you a mer-ry
2. Now bring us some fig-gy pud-ding, Now bring us some fig-gy

mf

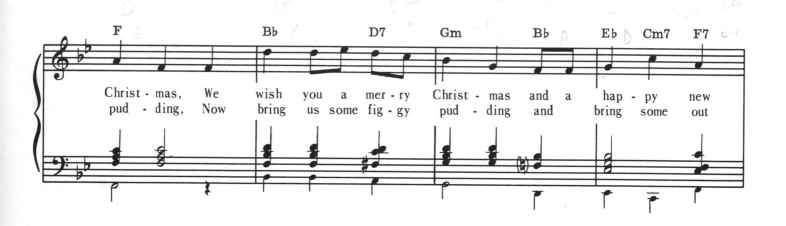

F — **Bb** — **D7** — **Gm** — **Bb** **Eb** **Cm7** **F7**

Christ-mas, We wish you a mer-ry Christ-mas and a hap-py new
pud-ding, Now bring us some fig-gy pud-ding and bring some out

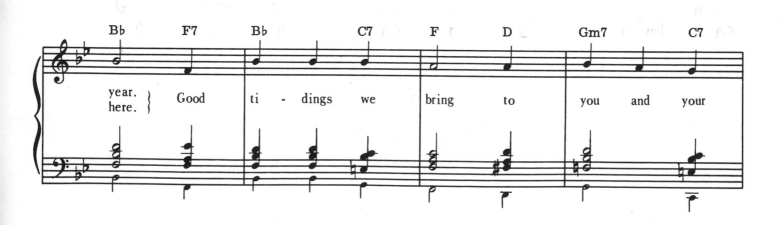

Bb **F7** **Bb** **C7** **F** **D** **Gm7** **C7**

year. } Good ti-dings we bring to you and your
here. }

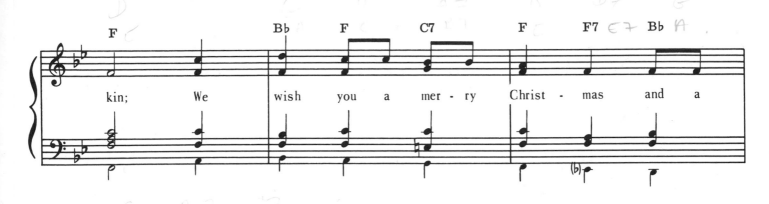

F   Bb   F   C7   F   F7   Bb

kin;   We   wish   you   a   mer - ry   Christ - mas   and   a

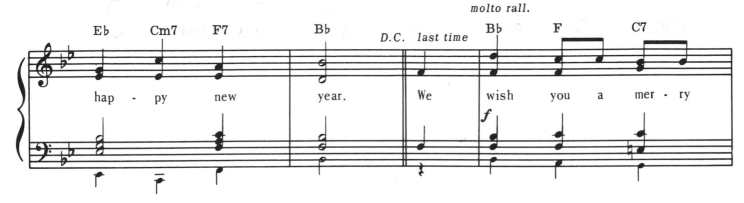

molto rall.

Eb   Cm7   F7   Bb   Bb   F   C7

hap - py   new   year.   We   wish   you   a   mer - ry

D.C. last time

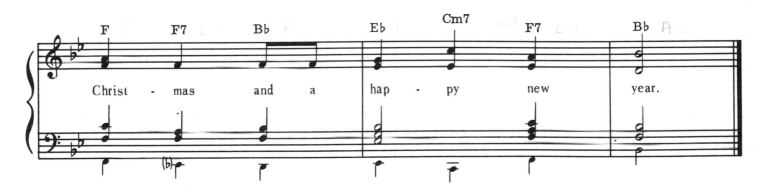

F   F7   Bb   Eb   Cm7   F7   Bb

Christ - mas   and   a   hap - py   new   year.

3.   For we all like figgy pudding,
       For we all like figgy pudding,
       For we all like figgy pudding,
       So bring some out here.
          Good tidings etc.

4.   And we won't go till we've got some,
       And we won't go till we've got some,
       And we won't go till we've got some,
       So bring some out here.
          Good tidings etc,

Registration No.	*Single-Manual Organs	*All Electronic Organs		*All Drawbar Organs	
1	8' 4' I II III	Upper: Lower: Pedal:	Flute 8' Melodia 8' 8', Soft	Upper: Lower: Pedal:	60 8808 000 (00) 5554 433 (1) 4-2 (Spinet 3)
2	8' I II	Upper: Lower: Pedal:	Cello 16', Trumpet 8', Flute 8', 4' Reed 8', Viola 8' (String 8') 16', 8', Full	Upper: Lower: Pedal:	40 8606 005 (00) 4543 222 (1) 4-2 (Spinet 3)
3	8' 2' I III V	Upper: Lower: Pedal:	Flute 16', (Tibia 16'), Clarinet 8', (Reed 8') Diapason 8' 16', Soft	Upper: Lower: Pedal:	60 8805 005 (00) 5544 321 (0) 4-2 (Spinet 3)
4	8' 4' 2' I II III V	Upper: Lower: Pedal:	Flute 16', (Tibia 16'), Flute 8' Diapason 8', Melodia 8' 16', 8' Medium	Upper: Lower: Pedal:	80 8080 800 (00) 6544 444 (2) 4-2 (Spinet 3)
5	8' 4' II	Upper: Lower: Pedal:	Flute 16', (Tibia 16'), Flute 8', Reed 8', Horn 8' Melodia 8', Diapason 8' 16', 8' Full	Upper: Lower: Pedal:	50 8806 006 (00) 5555 443 (3) 4-2 (Spinet 3)
6	8' 4' 2' I II V	Upper: Lower: Pedal:	Flute 16', (Tibia 16'), Flute 8', 4' Diapason 8', Horn 8' 16', 8' Medium	Upper: Lower: Pedal:	00 8080 600 (00) 4433 222 (0) 4-2 (Spinet 3)
7	8' II IV V	Upper: Lower: Pedal:	Diapason 8' Flute 8' 8' Medium	Upper: Lower: Pedal:	60 8008 000 (00) 5544 000 (0) 4-2 (Spinet 3)

* Vibrato and Reverberation left to personal preference